THE ONLY WAY OUT IS THROUGH

Essays

THE ONLY WAY OUT IS THROUGH

Katie Jean Shinkle

PART OF THE BLUE NOTE CHAPBOOK SERIES FROM YESYES BOOKS

COVER ART: "12 MARCH 25" © HOBBES GINSBERG, 2025. USED WITH PERMISSION.
DESIGN: KATIE PRINCE
PROJECT LEAD: KMA SULLIVAN
AUTHOR PHOTO: PJ CARLISLE

ISBN: 978-1-946303-12-7
PRINTED IN THE UNITED STATES OF AMERICA

PUBLISHED BY YESYES BOOKS
PORTLAND, OR
YESYESBOOKS.COM

(we can start over whenever we want to)

I SAY, FUCK THE BEES, KILL THEM ALL

But where would you keep her, / with all those huge strange thoughts in you / going and coming and sometimes staying the night? I say, fuck the bees, kill them all. What I mean is I am afraid. Bees, for me, are the only frightening insect, their flight and sound so painful. I use the word painful so often because language escapes me and I cannot find it. When I try to enter and re-enter it retreats, so fickle. *Who, if I cried out, would hear me among the angelic / orders?* I want to run far away when I hear wing movement, thorax muscles, an alarm of buzz. I am leaned up against the kitchen sink wiping my hands with a dishtowel and I say, god I hate bees so much. You immediately anger.

and at first, I am confused. I repeat myself, lost in a circle of language, an ouroboros of tongue and tail which makes you even angrier. This is what I do these days: get lost and cannot find my way out so I repeat and repeat until you crack. *For beauty is nothing / but the beginning of terror, which we can just barely endure.* I try to re-center and allow language to seep back in slowly, which it does at times when I am unprepared and ill-equipped such as this moment. I say, I don't give a shit about bees. There are 199 synonyms and antonyms in English for the word pain, but all I can access is one word. Short circuit. I wish I could say something, anything else. *Every angel is terrifying.*

and it is the first time I read poetry aloud to you, and you are so pissed off about the bees, but really you are pissed off at my retrieval of language, at my circular repetition, at my inability to articulate my thoughts or to communicate clearly. I am afraid of you X for no good reason. I am afraid of pain from a perceived threat of my own making. I am afraid of being a threat to myself and to others. I am afraid of hearing anything before I see it. I am afraid of colonies. I am afraid of the queen. I am afraid of the sting, the welt, the tears. I am afraid of even the idea of despair, of woe. This current exchange between us, filled to the brim with agony, the impending doom of trauma before it comes. The unpredictability. *Alas, whom can we turn to / in our need?*

and I want to say all of this to you. I want to apologize, even though I don't know what I am apologizing for. I want to ask, do you like being stung? Can I sting you in all your tender places? The heart in your chest and the heart tattooed on the inside of your arm? What of the welt it will leave, the tears surely on the brink? Even the word sting rolls out of my mouth like a song. What is the remedy for heartbreak? An epi pen? A mud pack, cool and grit? Baking soda? Do you still love me? How painful. I say fuck them bees. Your face gets red. I say, are you mad? I laugh. Your eyes never leave the TV. I sit next to you on the couch and open *The Duino Elegies*. I begin to read. I say, listen to these lines, *O and the night, the night, when the wind full of worldspace / gnaws at our faces--, for whom won't the night be there, / desired, gently disappointing, a hard rendezvous / for each toiling heart*. You shake your head, pause the video game, and say, *stop, I don't want to hear it. Stop it*. You go back to playing. A golden Sony PS4 controller in your hand, a jewel. You say *that is probably the most unintelligent thing you have ever said*. I halt mid-line. You clarify: About the bees. I finish: *Is it easier for lovers?*

and later in the deep evening, a crack and dust of snow silences the world outside. I am cradled in a blanket like a tomb, everything simultaneously cold and inviting. I will drink alone on the floor of our bathroom when you go out with your friends. Everyone is in town and wanting to see you. This is the first time I drink alone in our apartment—but not the last. I wait until you abandon the videogame, until you shout through the door *I'm leaving, be back later*. December and all along our silent street windows lit with twinkling lights of every color except ours. The clawfoot tub is unenclosed and I hit the top of my shoulders on the lips of the curved porcelain-enameled cast iron every time I lean back. I invite the pain. A momentary holiday in the air. I am drinking Christmas. The way pine scent is never actually pine scent, how juniper lies. I'm reading Rilke by myself: I'm reading about terror. I'm reading about yearning. About ghosts. About love. *Strange, to not go on wishing one's wishes.*

and I'm lying on the bathroom floor, tipping the bottle back into my mouth. I text a friend: there is something happening inside of me I find fascinating, a vast evening of insects inside of me. They text back: Sounds more like a snake, the longest of the world. Remember how the snake eats itself, less predictable than insects. I leave the empty pint of gin in the front pocket of my hoodie, tucked next to our bed, the most audacious secret. *Many a star was waiting / for your eyes only. A wave swelled toward you / out of the past, / or a violin surrendered itself / as you walked by an open window. All that was mission. / But were you up to it?*

(we can start over whenever we want can't we can't we we can start over whenever we want to
we can start over whenever we want can't we can't we we can start over whenever we want to
we can start over whenever we want can't we can't we we can start over whenever we want to
we can start over whenever we want can't we can't we we can start over whenever we want to
we can start over whenever we want can't we can't we we can start over whenever we want to)

There is a time before X I cannot remember clearly

A liminal space where nothing in memory presides

When it begins

A pile of ash

A tap from a blackened glass pipe

A pile of ash expands and expands, entire length of poplar, of cedar

A bookcase survived a house fire, now charred along top corner edges, tipped against the rough-
hewn wall of my apartment

A pile of ash   another   another   how the ash stains wood, resin smears

A time before X

overtaken by years

The marks on carpet permanent

Even with their mother's steam cleaner   even with soap and knees and scrub

I will get my deposit back and more

Poised as a restorative gift by the evil corporation who buy the building

The landlords kick everyone out

an increase in rent five times what I have paid

Tenants of the building 30 years

Weeping through walls

where will they go

X and I move in together two streets over

But before down-the-street   there is here

Ash on the bookshelf   an early sign of dismay

After our first date, I ask them not to post a picture of me. *Too soon,* I say. Instead, they post one picture: A stemmed glass of beer, a singular cigarette. The caption: This is my life, these are my choices. No mention of me (yet). No mention of us (yet). Only anticipation, excitement, rapture, potential love (never present in photographs).

The first time they yelled at me   over the ash on the bookshelf

over not being seen and heard

I kicked them out of my apartment   thought I would never speak to them again

My therapist tells me she is leaving the institution, *how did I feel?*
I said, *fine, my lover yelled at me last night*
over ash on my bookshelf   which was partially true   and partially not

The second-to-last appointment she had asked me if I thought I was a piece of shit.
She said *I think you fucking hate yourself and that it is why you act like you do   you think*
you are a piece of shit   who taught you that   whose voice is it   saying you are a piece of shit

A pile of ash

The time before X   I can't remember exactly   they were there

And then nothing else in my life mattered more   there was nothing else

The night after we are first together, I remember they called me, but I didn't answer
and the next afternoon I texted them and said: *Do you want to see me again?*
and they said: *Omfg, ofc, I thought about you all day, I just didn't want to bother you*

(we can start over whenever we want can't we can't we we can start over whenever we want to
we can start over whenever we want can't we can't we we can start over whenever we want to
we can start over whenever we want can't we can't we we can start over whenever we want to
we can start over whenever we want can't we can't we we can start over whenever we want to
we can start over whenever we want can't we can't we we can start over whenever we want to
we can start over whenever we want can't we can't we we can start over whenever we want to
we can start over whenever we want can't we can't we we can start over whenever we want to
we can start over whenever we want can't we can't we we can start over whenever we want to
we can start over whenever we want can't we can't we we can start over whenever we want to
we can start over whenever we want can't we can't we we can start over whenever we want to)

The first time I overdose on alcohol and give myself alcohol poisoning I am 14 years old. It is the first time I ever drink on pills with commitment. I black out in the middle of the day, half-clothed because I systematically take my clothes off running around my best friend's front yard. She is forced to re-dress me while I physically fight her. She will have a bruise on her arm for a week. She puts me in her bed to pass out. Lots of excuses to her mother and my mother made on why I am sick and not going home and sleeping at three in the afternoon on a random summer Tuesday. Close to midnight, I wake up in my own urine. My best friend and her boyfriend are watching a movie in the living room. They are making out and don't even look up when I stumble down the stairs to say I'm going home. I don't remember the entire afternoon. This behavior will be the pattern of a better part of my life. The drink snort smoke of a blackout. It will take 20 more years for me to find a better way through.

(we can start over whenever we want can't we can't we we can start over whenever we want to
we can start over whenever we want can't we can't we we can start over whenever we want to
we can start over whenever we want can't we can't we we can start over whenever we want to
we can start over whenever we want can't we can't we we can start over whenever we want to
we can start over whenever we want can't we can't we we can start over whenever we want to
we can start over whenever we want can't we can't we we can start over whenever we want to
we can start over whenever we want can't we can't we we can start over whenever we want to
we can start over whenever we want can't we can't we we can start over whenever we want to
we can start over whenever we want can't we can't we we can start over whenever we want to
we can start over whenever we want can't we can't we we can start over whenever we want to
we can start over whenever we want can't we can't we we can start over whenever we want to
we can start over whenever we want can't we can't we we can start over whenever we want to
we can start over whenever we want can't we can't we we can start over whenever we want to
we can start over whenever we want can't we can't we we can start over whenever we want to
we can start over whenever we want can't we can't we we can start over whenever we want to)

LATE AT NIGHT, RIGHT BEFORE SLEEP, I WORRY ABOUT THE KNIFE

as your fingers slip through. Sharp enough? Large or small enough? First, the crown chopped off, delicately placed to the side. Then halve through the core. You protect the fattest half in your hands, spindly skin to soft palm, to avoid impending doom. You run your index finger over the core's perfectly angular edge and it is here I think *sleep*. You set the palmed baby aside next to the gleaming muted leaves. You slide the knife through the other side of the core, liquid releases and streams down the edges of the cutting board. You gut the flesh. A perfect chunk. You say, *open your mouth. The first taste is always yours.* I close my eyes and wait. You lay the piece on my tongue like communion, letting your finger linger between my lips before I pucker around it and pull away. You turn your back to me as I chew, slice the core, rid the skin, gut the flesh, chop.

we can start over whenever we want can't we can't we we can start over whenever we want to

You say, *in so many other languages it's called ananas, but in English we brutalize the beauty, just like everything.* A sadness to every brutalization. I ask, *how do they grow?* You say, matter-of-factly, *pineapples grow pineapples.* You offer nothing else.

I ask myself today, how do pineapples grow? Answer: Exactly like we grow. Sever our heads. Let the crown fall. Plant us into the ground. Rebirth. Until we get it right.

we can start over whenever we want can't we can't we we can start over whenever we want to

At the end of our relationship, I sleep very little and shrink as small as I possibly can. Pineapples are the only fruit I will eat, otherwise I have banished all sources of sugar. I am folding into myself because I believe if I fold myself small enough maybe you will love me, and I am convinced of this, the smaller I am, the more I beg, you will love me the way I need you to love me.

Your website today says between this time and that time you were out in the "real world." In the real world was you & me. You loved me how you could. This I know for certain.

Before I am small, I am large, unwieldy. It is here you love me the most. The first time I bring home an expensive and out-of-season pineapple you do not chastise me. You lovingly take it out of the grocery bag and examine it. You pull the leaves out of the crown and teach me about ripeness. You cut the flesh and feed me. The first bite forever mine. Every time I came home with groceries, you would help put them away, no matter what you were doing. I would never ask. I never had to.

we can start over whenever we want can't we can't we we can start over whenever we want to

Endlessly, the late night, the pineapple. I plucked the leaves from the crown in the store. I lifted the edges to my nose in rapt inhale. A perfect fruit, almost spoiled. We must eat it before it rots away, before the sweetness betrays itself and turns to tang. We aren't sleeping, fits and starts. I ask you to cut the pineapple. I do not know the correct angle, how to remove the skin, the core, the symmetry. You do not want to tell me. You roll your eyes. You refuse. I say, tell me how and I will do it myself. I go to bed without putting the groceries away.

In the kitchen, you cut the fruit. I don't even know until I open the refrigerator in the morning and there it sits in a Tupperware. No first bites, no fingers through liquid, no witness of the pleasure of the lingering in sweet glut of flesh.

we can start over whenever we want can't we can't we we can start over whenever we want to

Eventually I stop asking for you to cut the pineapple.

Eventually I start buying it pre-cut from Whole Foods.

Eventually there is no longer pineapple in our apartment.

Eventually I stop eating pineapple.

we can start over whenever we want can't we can't we we can start over whenever we want to

Today you tell me you are okay, alright, but you aren't sleeping well. I wonder about how the ways we are unseen ultimately affects everything. I think about how small until miniscule I became so long ago, how little rest I needed in order to survive, us in the real world, your finger in my mouth, how the pineapple lost its allure. Years later I watched so many YouTube videos to learn to cut my own pineapple. My slices could be featured in a magazine, so perfect. How today I understand symmetry and shape and angles. How sharp the knife should be. Close your eyes, cradle the halves, rock yourself to sleep.

(we can start over whenever we want can't we can't we we can start over whenever we want to
we can start over whenever we want can't we can't we we can start over whenever we want to
we can start over whenever we want can't we can't we we can start over whenever we want to
we can start over whenever we want can't we can't we we can start over whenever we want to
we can start over whenever we want can't we can't we we can start over whenever we want to
we can start over whenever we want can't we can't we we can start over whenever we want to
we can start over whenever we want can't we can't we we can start over whenever we want to
we can start over whenever we want can't we can't we we can start over whenever we want to
we can start over whenever we want can't we can't we we can start over whenever we want to
we can start over whenever we want can't we can't we we can start over whenever we want to
we can start over whenever we want can't we can't we we can start over whenever we want to
we can start over whenever we want can't we can't we we can start over whenever we want to
we can start over whenever we want can't we can't we we can start over whenever we want to
we can start over whenever we want can't we can't we we can start over whenever we want to
we can start over whenever we want can't we can't we we can start over whenever we want to
we can start over whenever we want can't we can't we we can start over whenever we want to
we can start over whenever we want can't we can't we we can start over whenever we want to
we can start over whenever we want can't we can't we we can start over whenever we want to
we can start over whenever we want can't we can't we we can start over whenever we want to
we can start over whenever we want can't we can't we we can start over whenever we want to)

Symmetry and shape and angles.

Once, they asked me to post a picture of us at lunch and I compromised and agreed to take, but not post, a picture of them. A new job, a new promotion, they wanted me to say on the Internet I was proud of them. I put the phone down. I said, *I don't use the Internet that way.* We continued to lunch. They drank too much and didn't say a lot. I had hurt their feelings. Can I see them anymore? I am putting my phone back into my bag. I am biting my nails until I bleed. I am far away, out the window, across the city, out of the state, into space. I am trying to make myself smaller, to disappear. What am I saying now? My mouth won't stop but I have no idea what's coming out of it. I am watching myself from the ceiling. From outside of the window. From across the street. The moment, it's slipping. Has slipped. Is almost gone. As if the lack of curation can erase the coming heartbreak, as if the social media grid could show the truth somehow.

There are days my body is gutted, walking around see-through and incandescent, every organ punctured and leaking. Everything I touch is ruined. I wonder what kind of monster I am.

I have two photographs but no video from the apartment we shared: 600 sq/ft, one-bedroom in a restored Navy boarding house in the thick of the city.

Right before the break-up our bedroom in disarray in clutter, I'm cussing and kicking my belongings around. I say, *why do we live in such a small space? I don't understand. How did we get here?* And they say, *I was supposed to move in with you, but your landlord sold your building, and then we had to do something quickly, remember?*

I get mad for no reason and storm out to "take a walk" which usually means to go drink alone. I call my older brother and I wonder aloud if I have drug problem. He gently says, *I don't think so. You dabble, but its not a problem.* I do not ask if I have a drinking problem, which is also a drug problem. I say, *I feel like I need to go to rehab, this is taking its toll on me*. He says, *I really don't think you need it.* I sit on a brick overhang outside of a café across the street from my favorite marijuana dispensary. I let the sun soak into my face. I say, *yeah you're probably right.*

A few minutes later, I buy six airplane shots of whiskey from the liquor store eight blocks away from our apartment. I am not even out of the parking lot before I crack the seal on one and hide it in my fist under layers of zip-up hoodies and a North Face puffer coat. I am drunk by the time I get to the front steps our building.

When I gather the courage to enter, I go straight to bed. X is playing a video game with their headset on and doesn't even look up.

(we can start over whenever we want can't we can't we we can start over whenever we want to
we can start over whenever we want can't we can't we we can start over whenever we want to
we can start over whenever we want can't we can't we we can start over whenever we want to
we can start over whenever we want can't we can't we we can start over whenever we want to
we can start over whenever we want can't we can't we we can start over whenever we want to
we can start over whenever we want can't we can't we we can start over whenever we want to
we can start over whenever we want can't we can't we we can start over whenever we want to
we can start over whenever we want can't we can't we we can start over whenever we want to
we can start over whenever we want can't we can't we we can start over whenever we want to
we can start over whenever we want can't we can't we we can start over whenever we want to
we can start over whenever we want can't we can't we we can start over whenever we want to
we can start over whenever we want can't we can't we we can start over whenever we want to
we can start over whenever we want can't we can't we we can start over whenever we want to
we can start over whenever we want can't we can't we we can start over whenever we want to
we can start over whenever we want can't we can't we we can start over whenever we want to
we can start over whenever we want can't we can't we we can start over whenever we want to
we can start over whenever we want can't we can't we we can start over whenever we want to
we can start over whenever we want can't we can't we we can start over whenever we want to
we can start over whenever we want can't we can't we we can start over whenever we want to
we can start over whenever we want can't we can't we we can start over whenever we want to
we can start over whenever we want can't we can't we we can start over whenever we want to
we can start over whenever we want can't we can't we we can start over whenever we want to
we can start over whenever we want can't we can't we we can start over whenever we want to
we can start over whenever we want can't we can't we we can start over whenever we want to
we can start over whenever we want can't we can't we we can start over whenever we want to)

We decide to go to Chili's for dinner, and I am unsure why we are going to Chili's when we live in a city with better food options. We both order margaritas. I never drink margaritas because they give me heartburn. I won't recognize what heartburn is until I stop drinking alcohol for good. I drink my drink fast, but the drink is not quite finished, and I'm already perusing the drink menu for another.

They say, *Why don't you just enjoy the drink in front of you? Why are you already ordering another one?*

I say, *because I can't just have one. That's not how it works.*

They are on their phone and won't look me in the eye. I lick the spicy-salt rim of the glass in silence.

Can I get another drink? I ask. *Do you care?*

They say, *You're a grown-up, you don't have to ask permission. You know that's not what this is about.*

I say, *Then what is it about.*

They start furiously texting. Who are they texting? I order another drink. Another. Another. Another. Another. I am weeping at the table before we leave. I stumble on the way to the car. I hold in my puke until we get home.

I'm honest from the first day of our relationship about who I am. I take pride in the fact I do not hide, until I do. I don't want to hide anymore, and so it is here at the crossroads of the relationship where I want to tell the real truth. I want to lay my burden down. I want to confess about how much pain I am in. How my spirit is dead. How the lights inside are turned off. How I need help. It feels like everything is falling apart.

(we can start over whenever we want can't we can't we we can start over whenever we want to
we can start over whenever we want can't we can't we we can start over whenever we want to
we can start over whenever we want can't we can't we we can start over whenever we want to
we can start over whenever we want can't we can't we we can start over whenever we want to
we can start over whenever we want can't we can't we we can start over whenever we want to
we can start over whenever we want can't we can't we we can start over whenever we want to
we can start over whenever we want can't we can't we we can start over whenever we want to
we can start over whenever we want can't we can't we we can start over whenever we want to
we can start over whenever we want can't we can't we we can start over whenever we want to
we can start over whenever we want can't we can't we we can start over whenever we want to
we can start over whenever we want can't we can't we we can start over whenever we want to
we can start over whenever we want can't we can't we we can start over whenever we want to
we can start over whenever we want can't we can't we we can start over whenever we want to
we can start over whenever we want can't we can't we we can start over whenever we want to
we can start over whenever we want can't we can't we we can start over whenever we want to
we can start over whenever we want can't we can't we we can start over whenever we want to
we can start over whenever we want can't we can't we we can start over whenever we want to
we can start over whenever we want can't we can't we we can start over whenever we want to
we can start over whenever we want can't we can't we we can start over whenever we want to
we can start over whenever we want can't we can't we we can start over whenever we want to
we can start over whenever we want can't we can't we we can start over whenever we want to
we can start over whenever we want can't we can't we we can start over whenever we want to
we can start over whenever we want can't we can't we we can start over whenever we want to
we can start over whenever we want can't we can't we we can start over whenever we want to
we can start over whenever we want can't we can't we we can start over whenever we want to
we can start over whenever we want can't we can't we we can start over whenever we want to
we can start over whenever we want can't we can't we we can start over whenever we want to
we can start over whenever we want can't we can't we we can start over whenever we want to
we can start over whenever we want can't we can't we we can start over whenever we want to
we can start over whenever we want can't we can't we we can start over whenever we want to)

When we reconnect years later the relationship feels *a lifetime ago*, X says, *but I know it wasn't all that long*. This confession feels like a dismissal, as if the relationship wasn't significant or impactful. My feelings are hurt. Yes, a lifetime ago. What remains? Possibly the sorrow in refusing participation in the living archive of our love, the wedge of absence of intimacy. The years we were together, I let them take very few photos of me. I could not stand to look at myself and certainly I did not want to be seen through the eyes of the Other. Deep down I did not want documentation of my downfall. The drinking, the bottom. I refused to be perceived in any tangible way by my lover, by the outside. All photos had to be curated by me. I was attempting to control the narrative. They were not allowed to post photos to the Internet without my permission, and they obliged. There was, at first, a sense of empathy in honoring my request, and then there is a sense of resignation, and finally a sense of shame, which I now recognize as deep insecurity. The final undoing.

TAKE A PICTURE OF ME, I'LL TAKE A PICTURE OF YOU, AND TOGETHER WE'LL DEVELOP INTO

the way we can re-imagine the Other. This way, apart from each other so wholly, the Other only exists in what remains as reverb. Wah-wah pedal. A sizzling static across time and space. In the deepest pit of our stomachs. No, below that. No, lower still. The Other my X crouched in darkness.

Close your eyes. Think of us. What do you see? Can you see us anymore?

A curious facet of the Internet is the illusion that one's life can be scrubbed clean through the curation of social media accounts, free of our pasts. If only this were true, we could deliver ourselves with a simple delete and trash (and delete the trash again for good measure). I put my friends on the investigative case before I can ever bring myself to. One reports back X's Instagram only holds two pictures of us and in a screenshot I see. My Instagram holds none, wiped as if the relationship never existed. Years of togetherness decidedly lost in the ether of ghost-time. I remember how easygoing the act of removal and excavation was for me, sidelined in grief, fully committed to a narrative of moving on. Here I am in the cognitive dissonance of simultaneity. We are here now, and we are still together, then. My therapist said if I don't deal with my own reckoning, it will follow me until I do. The act of forgetting is not easy.

In my tagged photos is where the narrative of our once-life-together lives. Objects. Shadows. Ambiance. Environs. Our shared dog I begged not to adopt when I was in the middle of writing my Ph.D. dissertation. I will never see the dog again in real life and my heart aches for that little animal. Here I am haunting the year we leave each other. I'm sitting on our couch crouched into myself, my head in my arms, our dog chewing on my shirt, wishing X would truly see me. Fast forward and I'm sitting on my spouse's and my couch curled into myself, my head in my arms, scrolling, lost inside memory. It is here I blame X's disinterest as the reason we have no documentation of our physical bodies in time and place together. But then I remember: this is my fault. I refused photographs.

Think of me. What do you see? Can you see me anymore? Close your eyes.

All the between spaces of days the Instagram grid never lets us in on. A photo of our shadows in the park walking the dog, one of few showing our physical proximity to each other. We were arguing over beer bottles, where I put my ash from my glass pipe, that I didn't wake up until 2:00PM. Our shadows lean in and disguise the fight. A photo of mason jars filled with roses and baby's breath, lit votive candles, light's reflection off glass, the never warm radiator of our apartment in the background. It is our last Valentine's Day and X perfected Ina Garten's roasted chicken and angel food cake which I worry they make for other people now. X practiced the week before at their parents' house to perfect the recipes. I never saw this as love but simply lack which was so wrong of me. What the photo doesn't show is our fight about how they barely acknowledged the accomplishment of my Ph.D. achievement. They were jealous, immature. There was no celebration. What the photo doesn't show is the pain, the grief, the relationship finally coming to an end long after it should have.

My therapist said *you didn't want your picture taken because you hated yourself.* She said *you hate yourself because you think you are a piece of shit. Whose voice is that? The one that says you are a piece of shit. You learned it somewhere, and you have to unlearn it.*

Can you see me anymore?

Close your eyes. Think of me.

What do you see?

We stand in front of the mirror behind their produce display, the waterfall effect cascading down to a perfect triangle, multiple pyramids, the sands of time and abracadabra. They take the phone out of their work apron and I wince. I think they are going to take a picture of me. *I'm not going to take a picture of you, Jesus Christ babe* they say shaking their head in annoyance. They are taking a picture of their display instead—the cull and shine and stack. I am angry at this response, but how can I be? The disseverment growing deeper with every picture not taken, not posted.

My therapist says *loving yourself before you can love someone else? It's bullshit.*

Close your eyes. Think of me.

I take a photo, and the shadow has shifted. I try another and the light is no longer perfect, but something remains. I take another. I take 100 more. I have gold chains and red lipstick on, same as I ever was. Here X let us take a picture together in the fantasy of us. A super rupture of time and space. Then & now. Where we live into perpetuity. Our amends like flash. Your arm through mine. A celebration. My eyes open. What do I see? I post the photo, us laughing, us kissing, us into a future that never existed. I will keep posting forever & ever & ever.

we can start over whenever we want can't we can't we we can start over whenever we want to
we can start over whenever we want can't we can't we we can start over whenever we want to
we can start over whenever we want can't we can't we we can start over whenever we want to
we can start over whenever we want can't we can't we we can start over whenever we want to
we can start over whenever we want can't we can't we we can start over whenever we want to
we can start over whenever we want can't we can't we we can start over whenever we want to
we can start over whenever we want can't we can't we we can start over whenever we want to
we can start over whenever we want can't we can't we we can start over whenever we want to
we can start over whenever we want can't we can't we we can start over whenever we want to
we can start over whenever we want can't we can't we we can start over whenever we want to
we can start over whenever we want can't we can't we we can start over whenever we want to
we can start over whenever we want can't we can't we we can start over whenever we want to
we can start over whenever we want can't we can't we we can start over whenever we want to
we can start over whenever we want can't we can't we we can start over whenever we want to
we can start over whenever we want can't we can't we we can start over whenever we want to
we can start over whenever we want can't we can't we we can start over whenever we want to
we can start over whenever we want can't we can't we we can start over whenever we want to
we can start over whenever we want can't we can't we we can start over whenever we want to
we can start over whenever we want can't we can't we we can start over whenever we want to
we can start over whenever we want can't we can't we we can start over whenever we want to
we can start over whenever we want can't we can't we we can start over whenever we want to
we can start over whenever we want can't we can't we we can start over whenever we want to
we can start over whenever we want can't we can't we we can start over whenever we want to
we can start over whenever we want can't we can't we we can start over whenever we want to
we can start over whenever we want can't we can't we we can start over whenever we want to
we canstart over whenever we want can't we can't we we can start over whenever we want to
we can start over whenever we want can't we can't we we can start over whenever we want to
we can start over whenever we want can't we can't we we can start over whenever we want to
we can start over whenever we want can't we can't we we can start over whenever we want to
we can start over whenever we want can't we can't we we can start over whenever we want to
we can start over whenever we want can't we can't we we can start over whenever we want to
we can start over whenever we want can't we can't we we can start over whenever we want to
we can start over whenever we want can't we can't we we can start over whenever we want to
we can start over whenever we want can't we can't we we can start over whenever we want to
we can start over whenever we want can't we can't we we can start over whenever we want to
we can start over whenever we want can't we can't we we can start over whenever we want to
we can start over whenever we want can't we can't we we can start over whenever we want to
we can start over whenever we want can't we can't we we can start over whenever we want to

I take a photo, and it is perfect.

NOTES

In "I say, fuck the bees, kill them all" lines quoted from "The First Elegy," Rainer Maria Rilke. (Rilke, Rainer Maria. *Duino Elegies*. Translated by Edward Snow. North Point Press, 2000.)

Thank you to the following editors and magazines, where some of these essays first appeared: *Gulf Coast, South Dakota Review, Hunger Mountain.*

ALSO BY YESYES BOOKS

FICTION

The Nothing by Lauren Davis
Girls Like Me by Nina Packebush
Three Queerdos and a Baby by Nina Packebush
Book of Exemplary Women by Diana Xin

WRITING RESOURCES

Gathering Voices: Creating a Community-Based Poetry Workshop by Marty McConnell

FULL-LENGTH POETRY COLLECTIONS

Ugly Music by Diannely Antigua
Bone Language by Jamaica Baldwin
Cataloguing Pain by Allison Blevins
Strange Flowers by Bryan Byrdlong
What Runs Over by Kayleb Rae Candrilli
Don't Cut Your Own Bangs by Caroline Crew
This, Sisyphus by Brandon Courtney
Salt Body Shimmer by Aricka Foreman
Gutter by Lauren Brazeal Garza
Forever War by Kate Gaskin
Inconsolable Objects by Nancy Miller Gomez
Ceremony of Sand by Rodney Gomez
Undoll by Tanya Grae
Loudest When Startled by luna rey hall
Everything Breaking / For Good by Matt Hart
Brine Orchid by Arah Ko
40 WEEKS by Julia Kolchinsky
murmurations by Anthony Thomas Lombardi
Sons of Achilles by Nabila Lovelace
Refusenik by Lynn Melnick
GOOD MORNING AMERICA I AM HUNGRY AND ON FIRE by jamie mortara
Born Backwards by Tanya Olson

a falling knife has no handle by Emily O'Neill
To Love an Island by Ana Portnoy Brimmer
Another Way to Split Water by Alycia Pirmohamed
Tell This to the Universe by Katie Prince
One God at a Time by Meghan Privitello
I'm So Fine: A List of Famous Men & What I Had On by Khadijah Queen
If the Future Is a Fetish by Sarah Sgro
Gilt by Raena Shirali
[insert] boy by Danez Smith
Say It Hurts by Lisa Summe
Hand Over Hand Over the Edge of the World by Patrick Swaney
Boat Burned by Kelly Grace Thomas
Helen Or My Hunger by Gale Marie Thompson
As She Appears by Shelley Wong

RECENT CHAPBOOK COLLECTIONS

Vinyl 45s

- *carried / in our own language* by Tatiana Dolgushina
- *Exit Pastoral* by Aidan Forster
- *Crown for the Girl Inside* by Lisa Low
- *Phantasmagossip* by Sara Mae
- *Year of the Sheep* by Stacey Park
- *Scavenger* by Jessica Lynn Suchon
- *Unmonstrous* by John Allen Taylor
- *Giantess* by Emily Vizzo

Blue Note Editions

- *Kissing Caskets* by Mahogany L. Browne
- *One Above One Below: Positions & Lamentations* by Gala Mukomolova
- *The Porch (As Sanctuary)* by Jae Nichelle

www.ingramcontent.com/pod-product-compliance
Lightning Source LLC
LaVergne TN
LVHW080318110826
845155LV00023B/134

* 9 7 8 1 9 4 6 3 0 3 1 2 7 *